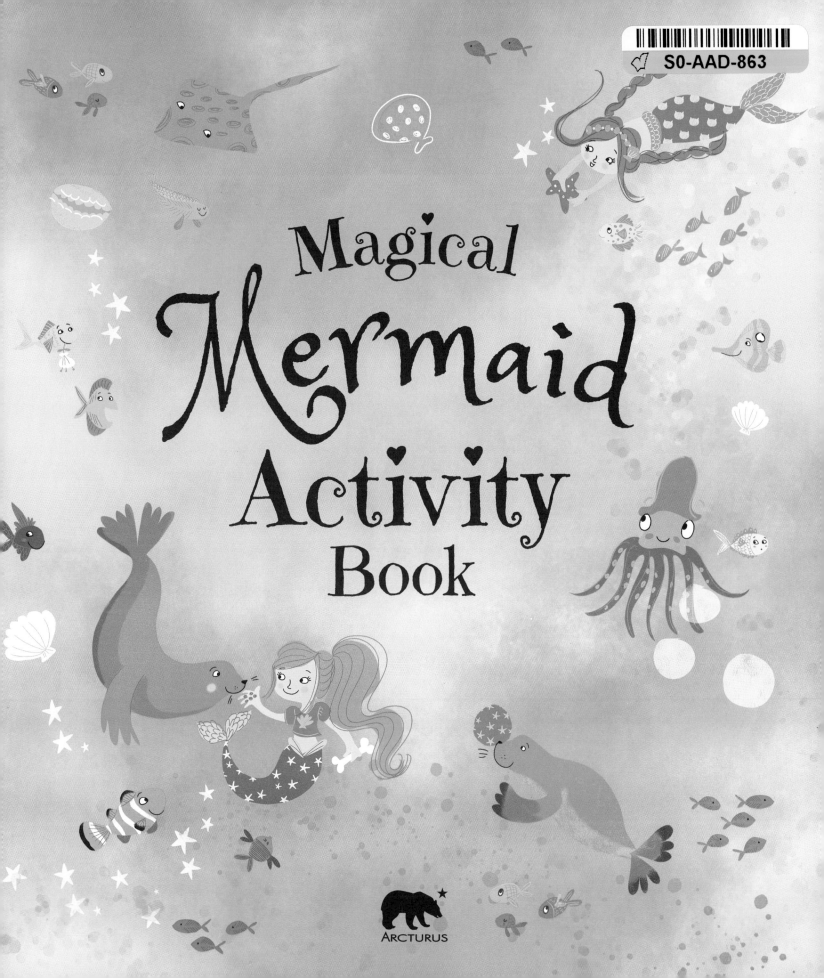

Magical Mermaid Activity Book

ARCTURUS

ARCTURUS

This edition published in 2020 by Arcturus Publishing Limited
26/27 Bickels Yard, 151–153 Bermondsey Street,
London SE1 3HA

Illustrated by Samantha Loman
Written by Lisa Regan
Edited by Susannah Bailey
Designed by Well Nice Ltd

ISBN: 978-1-78888-156-2
CH006434NT
Supplier 29, Date 0620, Print run 10352
Distributed by LTD Commodities

Printed in China

Say Hello!

Unscramble the letters to find out the names of these four friendly mermaids.

ORCAL

A

AREPL

B

HYLELS

QAUA

C

D

Under the Sea

Welcome to the mermaids' watery world!
Can you spot the items shown below?

Beautiful Babies

These playful dolphins are returning to their mothers. Can you follow the lines to pair them back up?

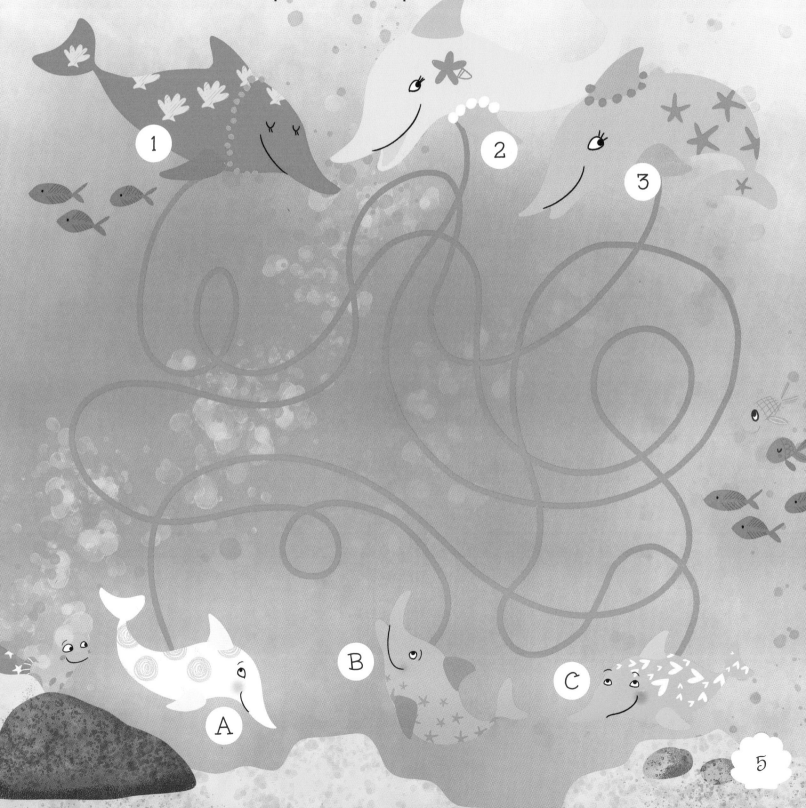

Gift Giving

Aqua is making a necklace for her friend, Pearl. Study the pattern, and work out which two shells she needs to thread onto the end.

A B C D

Party Time

Bring this underwater party to life with lots of blues, greens, and pretty pinks.

What's Your Mermaid Name?

Answer the questions and follow the arrows to find out!

START

Sleepover or skate party?

Jogging or swimming?

Glitter or grunge?

Lie-in or up and about?

TV or talking?

Spots or stripes?

Ponytail or let it loose?

Dolphins or sharks?

Singing or Dancing?

Gold or silver?

Stars or the Moon?

Reading or gaming?

Smoothie or Milkshake?

Your name is...
Calypso
"Sea Nymph"

Your name is...
Aurora
"the Dawn"

Your name is...
Merissa
"Sea Lover"

8

Stormy Seas

Take a look at these two pictures, and try to spot eight differences between them.

Bobbing Along

Match these cute seahorses into pairs. Which seahorse doesn't have one?

Secret Message

Fill in all the boxes that contain the letters S, E, and A.
The remaining letters spell a message from Coral and Shelly.

E	S	A	S	S	A	E	E	S	A
A	E	S	E	E	S	E	A	A	E
S	E	S	J	E	O	A	I	E	N
A	E	E	E	S	A	S	E	A	S
E	S	O	S	U	E	R	S	A	S
A	E	A	E	A	S	A	S	E	E
E	S	E	E	S	A	S	A	E	S
S	A	S	F	A	U	A	N	A	E
S	S	E	A	S	A	S	E	A	S
E	E	A	S	A	A	E	A	S	A

11

Seeing Stars

The mermaids are star-hunting in this shipwreck scene.
How many are there? Remember to look for all types of star!

Round and Round

Find out what this octopus is called by circling every other letter from left to right, starting at the top. These letters spell her name. The first one has been done for you.

O
O S
S T
Q I
B
U
G R E T
G

S _ _ _ _ _ _ _ _

Coco the Clown

Coco is another of the mermaids' friends.
He looks a lot like the other clownfish, but not
exactly the same. Where is he?

Magical Mer-king

Which of the jigsaw pieces below completes the royal scene?

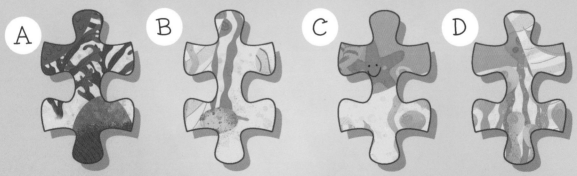

A   B   C   D

Undersea Creatures

Can you find these swimming sea creatures hidden in the grid?
Words can be found forward, backward, and diagonally.

DOLPHIN **CRAB** **OCTOPUS** **FISH**

S	E	A	N	O	I	L	A	E	S
S	D	O	L	P	H	I	N	S	F
H	E	W	E	R	P	N	C	R	I
E	C	A	T	H	C	A	E	C	S
L	A	R	H	P	R	B	A	U	H
A	B	S	A	O	T	E	U	C	B
H	S	O	L	B	R	L	S	O	O
W	R	P	L	O	B	S	T	E	R
P	R	T	S	W	L	S	E	P	O
S	U	P	O	T	C	O	T	S	B

SEAHORSE **WHALE** **LOBSTER**

SEALION

17

Golden Bells and Pearl Shells

Welcome to the royal palace! How many golden bells and pearl shells can you count in this picture?

BELL

SHELL

18

Wavy Hair!

Pearl is washing her beautiful, long curls. Which of her shadows exactly matches the main picture?

Mer-maze

Can you help Coral avoid the eels on her way back to the palace?

Shell Sorting

Sort these special, magic shells into groups that are the same.
Which type are there most of? Which is the smallest group?

Home Sweet Home

Copy this picture of the underwater palace, and then decorate it with your pens or crayons.

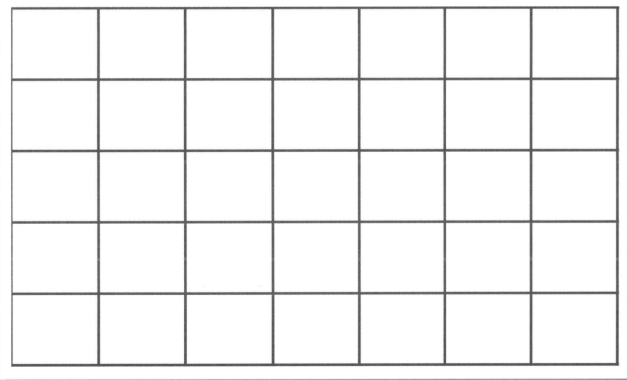

Missing Link

Cross out any letter that appears twice. The leftover letters spell the name of a shelled sea creature. Which one is it?

A P L W
O W B F
   T F P
S
E   R A

Shining Bright

Can you find this line of four jewels somewhere in the large pattern?

Lost and Found

Which of the treasure chests is the one the prince is looking for? Use the clues to work it out.

It has a lock on it.

It has a flat lid.

It has handles.

It contains a golden goblet.

Watery words

How many smaller words can you make, using the letters from HIDDEN TREASURE?
Write them down as you think of them.

HIDDEN TREASURE

Wonderful Whales

Pick up your pens, and finish these amazing creatures with beautiful patterns.

28

Starry Night

Shelly loves to swim to the surface at night, and gaze at the stars.
Can you spot this constellation?

Seadoku

Use the pictures above the grid to fill in the blank spaces.
You must arrange them so that each line across, each line down, and
each mini-grid has just one of each picture.

Mermaid Song

Can you find a musical note that appears only once on this page?

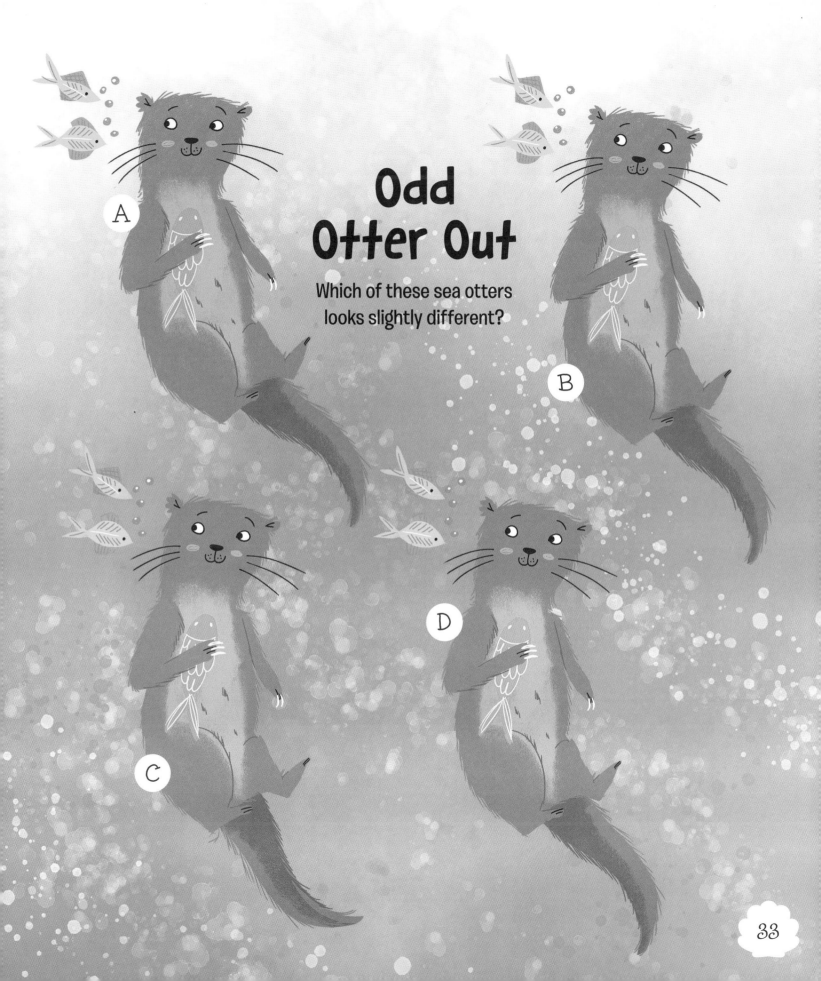

Odd Otter Out

Which of these sea otters looks slightly different?

Mer-map

Use the grid on the map to answer the questions.
For example, the turtles are in square 2B.

1. Look at square 4C.
How many mermaids are there?

....

2. Find squares 5B, 5C, and 5D.
Where is the octopus?

....

3. Is there a whale or
a shark in 2E?

....

4. Which letter is on the row
where the dolphins play?

....

5. Which square contains the
Mer-king: 3A, 2E, or 4B?

....

6. What creature is in 3A?

....

7. If you want to visit the
palace, should you go to 1B?

....

8. Which column has the most
mermaids in it: 1, 3, or 4?

....

Crab Course

Help Chloe the crab scuttle from start to finish by jumping on a pink shell, then
a green one, then a purple one, repeating the pattern the whole way.
She can only move downward and from side to side.

Masterclass

Follow the step-by-step pictures to create your very own mermaid!

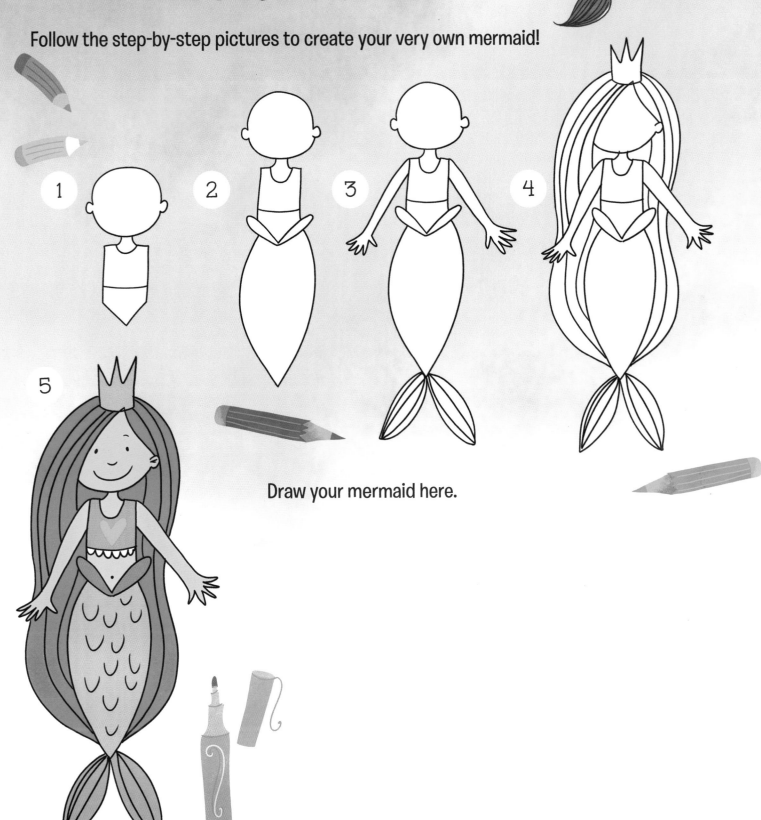

Draw your mermaid here.

Magical Unicorns

The mermaids love to leave the water, to see what's happening on the land. Can you help the mermaids find Shimmer, their special unicorn friend? She has a purple horn and purple hooves.

Cool Creatures

Go wild with your pens and crayons to make
these creatures and plants even more amazing!

Mermaid Whispers

It's so much fun playing games with your friends!
For this one, you'll need at least four of you, sitting in a line.

The person at one end (let's imagine it is you) thinks of something silly to say.
Try something like:

"Many of the mermaids get the giggles when they gossip."

Whisper it to the person sitting next to you. That person then whispers the message to the next person, but it has to be done immediately, with no thinking time, and you can only hear the message once.

Work to the end of the line, passing the message on quickly. There is a big chance that the message you end up with won't be anything like the original!

Tangled Tiaras

Oops! Aqua has got her tiaras in a big muddle.
Can you count how many there are on the page?

Mirror, Mirror

These gorgeous mer-mirrors have all been found in the sand. They seem the same, but one of them is slightly different. Can you find it?

A

B

C

D

E

Wild Waves

Fill this page with waves, swirls, and pretty patterns, to remind you of the majestic ocean.

Find the Friends

The mermaids have lots of creatures to play with under the sea.
Look at the list, and then find all of them in the picture.

- pink octopus
- crab
- turtle
- sea snail
- merboy
- clownfish
- lobster
- blacktip shark

Splash!

Each of the dolphins has at least one identical friend, except one.
Can you find it?

Custom Made

Get creative with your pens and crayons to finish designing these beautiful accessories.

Finders Keepers

Lots of pretty keys have sunk to the bottom of the ocean over the years!
Link each one to its pair, and find one that doesn't have a match.

Criss Cross

Which purse belongs to Shelly?
Join the dots in order to cross out all except one of them.

Otter Spotter

Can you find this adorable baby otter in the crowd?

Super-search

Look for all the mermaids' magical friends hidden in this wordsearch grid. Words can be found forward, backward, and diagonally.

P	T	N	A	I	G	O	N
I	C	G	C	E	N	R	O
X	G	E	R	F	F	O	G
I	I	N	N	I	L	G	A
E	A	I	E	T	A	E	R
U	N	E	L	N	A	N	D
N	F	A	I	R	Y	U	N
U	N	I	C	O	R	N	R

PIXIE

FAIRY

ELF

GIANT

DRAGON

CENTAUR

UNICORN

GENIE

Ring, Ring!

Which of these beautiful gems does Shelly find in her treasure box?
Use the clues to work it out.

1. It contains at least one red stone.

2. It doesn't have any green stones on it.

3. It has three stones on it.

4. It contains at least one pink stone.

5. It doesn't have any blue stones.

Bubble Trouble

Find a way through the bubble maze to get to Casey the crab.

START

FINISH

Gem-tastic

Look carefully in the large grid to find this pattern of gems there.

Dressing Up

The mermaids are having a great time trying on each other's outfits!
Decorate them with your pens and crayons.

Time for Bed

Can you spot six differences between these two pictures?

Twinkly Tiaras

Which two beautiful tiaras are exactly the same?

MAGICAL MUSIC

Melody is playing a beautiful tune for all of her friends.
Can you see which silhouette is exactly the same shape as the picture?

Pretty Patterns

Look along each line and work out what comes next to fill the spaces.

1

2

3

4

Quiz Time

Which of the mermaids would you have as your BFF?
Answer the questions and keep count of the letters you pick as you go along.

1. Do you prefer clothes in shades of?

A. Pink.

B. Purple.

C. Blue.

D. Yellow.

2. Which of these do you enjoy the most?

A. Chatting.

B. Reading.

C. TV.

D. Drawing.

3. What creature would you like as a pet?

A. A dog or a cat.

B. A mouse or a fish.

C. A tortoise or a lizard.

D. A gerbil or a hamster.

4. What would your friends say is the best thing about you?

A. You are funny.

B. You are kind.

C. You are generous.

D. You are smart.

5. How do you wear your hair at the weekend?

A. clipped away from your eyes.

B. in a bun.

C. loose and flowing.

D. all ways-weekends are for experimenting!

6. What kind of job would you like when you're grown up?

A. Working with animals.

B. Something creative.

C. Working with people.

D. Something brainy.

7. Who knows more of your secrets than anyone?

A. Your mother.

B. Your best friend.

C. Your father.

D. Only your diary knows ...

Results

Mostly As

You and Coral would get along swimmingly! She loves exciting things—parties, music, fashion—the brighter and bolder the better! You are probably one of the first in your group to get noticed, but that's fine by you!

Mostly Bs

Shelly is your shoal-mate! You both love to be in a crowd, and are happiest when you're surrounded by friends and family. The only things that really make you sad are being lonely, or others being unkind.

Mostly Cs

You're like Aqua—calm, sweet, and gentle. She is always willing to lend a helping hand, and that is one of your best qualities, too. We hope your friends appreciate what a lovely person you are!

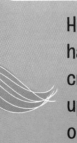

Mostly Ds

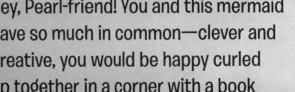

Hey, Pearl-friend! You and this mermaid have so much in common—clever and creative, you would be happy curled up together in a corner with a book or a sketchpad.

Shell Seeker

Can you find a shell that looks like this, somewhere in the sand?

Fishy Friends

Copy these happy fish, then decorate them with your pens or pencils.

Celebrations

Which of these birthday cakes does Aqua want for her party?
Use the clue to find out!

1. It isn't heart-shaped.

2. It doesn't have any rainbow sprinkles.

3. It is decorated with starfish.

4. It has shells on top.

A

B

D

C

E

Party time

Can you find the three framed sections, somewhere in the party scene?

1

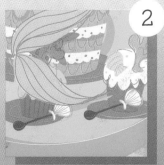

2

3

Unique Fish

Which butterflyfish doesn't have a twin?

Remember, Remember

Take a good look at this scene, remembering as much as you can.
Then turn the page and test your memory!

Remember, Remember

Can you remember what you saw? Write down
everything you can!

1. Which animal was in the tree?

....

2. How many mermaids were swimming?

....

3. Which two of these butterflies did
you see?

A   B   C

4. Which creature is sitting on a
mermaid's lap?

....

5. What do the toadstools look like?

A   B   C

6. Who is flying in the sky?

....

7. Which of these mermaids has her
hands in her hair?

A   B   C

8. Are the rabbits white or brown?

....

Treasure Trove

Can you find all the precious things that Pearl stores in her chest? Words can be found forward, backward, and diagonally.

PEARL

DIAMOND

OPAL

RUBY

R	D	I	P	E	N	G	W
U	N	A	E	E	N	R	C
B	O	E	A	I	A	W	R
E	M	E	R	A	L	D	O
M	A	N	L	U	A	E	W
T	I	A	R	A	B	A	N
R	D	I	L	S	B	Y	R
E	E	R	E	L	A	P	O

RING

TIARA

CROWN

EMERALD

69

Ocean Rescue

The mermaids have saved a prince who was lost in a storm! He wanted to take a picture to remember them. Can you spot six differences between the two pictures?

Join in!

Add more fabulous fish to the scene, and finish it with your pens and crayons.

Get Creative!

What has happened here? Write a story based on the pictures. It can be whatever you want, so use your imagination!

....

....

....

....

....

....

....

....

....

....

....

Sort It Out

What a mess! Can you help Little Squirt figure out which of the anchors is attached to each boat?

A

B

C

1

2

3

Giddy Up!

Coral is having a great time riding her special sea horse.
Which of the silhouette outlines matches the main picture?

Watch Out!

Can you find six sneaky sharks hiding in this scene?

Mer-map

Use the grid on the map to answer the questions. For example, the mountains are in squares 1B and 2B.

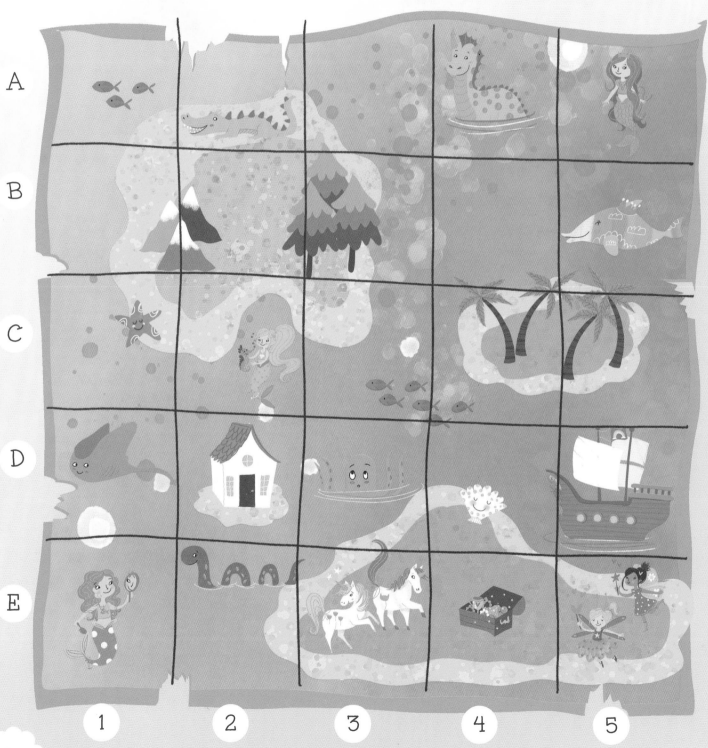

1. Look at square 5B.
What creature is there?

....

2. Is the friendly crocodile in
1A, 2A, or 3A?

....

3. How many trees are in 5C?

....

4. Where is the pine forest?

....

5. Is the smallest island in
row B, D, or E?

....

6. What creatures are in 3E?

....

7. Which square does not contain a
magical sea monster: 4A, 4D, or 2E?

....

8. Which square contains fairies:
5B, 5D, or 5E?

....

Scaredy Fish

Something has frightened poor Bubbles the puffer fish!
See if you can spot eight difference between the two pictures.

Pattern Mad

Copy this picture of the friendly whale, and then decorate it with your pens or pencils.

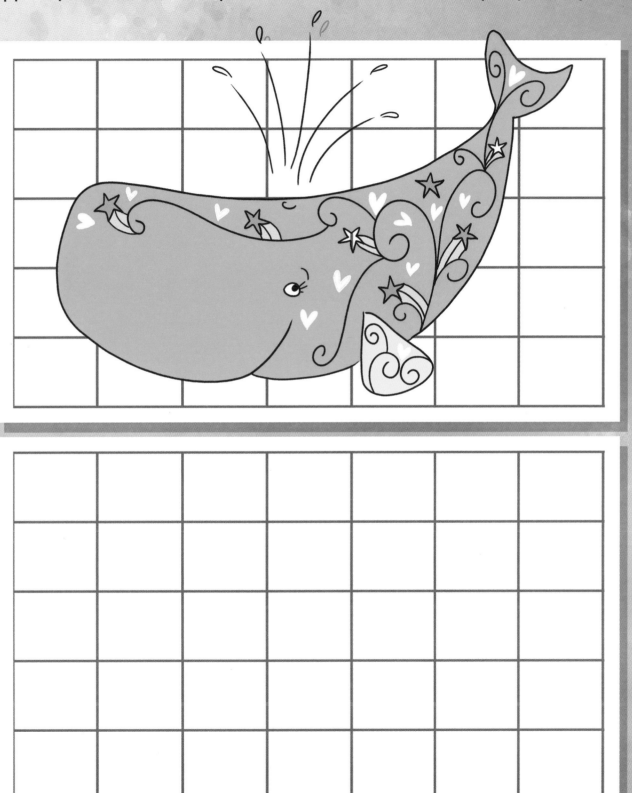

I Love Mermaids

Look carefully to find a single green heart, hidden in the mermaid's tail.

80

Wide-eyed Crab

Follow the step-by-step pictures to draw your very own crab!

Try drawing a crab here.

Sea Tridents

The Mer-king is counting his tridents, but they keep floating away! Can you keep track of how many there are?

Help for Kelpie

Can you find Kelpie the sea horse a way out of the rainbow maze?

Cute Shell-fie!

These BFFs have printed shell-fies!
Which one of them is a tiny bit different from the others?

Looking Out

What can Shelly see from her window? You decide, then add it to the picture and complete it with pens and pencils.

Pearl's Purse

Where has Pearl left her purse?
See if you can find it for her.

Magical Mermaid Activity Book

Answers

Answers

Page 3: Say Hello!
A Coral, B Pearl, C Aqua, D Shelly

Page 4: Under the Sea

Page 5: Beautiful Babies
1 A, 2 C, 3 B

Page 6: Gift Giving
A, A

Page 9: Stormy Seas

Page 10: Bobbing Along

Page 11: Secret Message
JOIN OUR FUN

Pages 12-13: Seeing Stars
28

Page 14: Round and Round
Squirt

Page 15: Coco the Clown

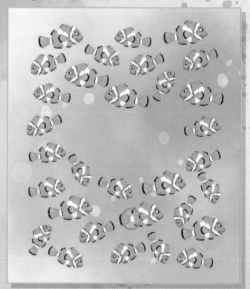

Answers

Page 16: Magical Mer-king
D

Page 17: Undersea Creatures

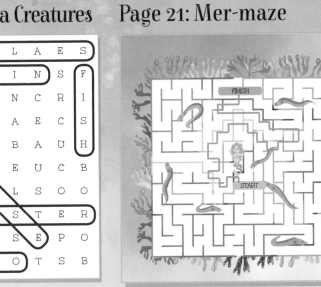

Pages 18–19: Golden Bells and Pearl Shells
Golden bells: 7. Pearl shells: 14.

Page 20: Wavy Hair
C

Page 21: Mer-maze

Page 22: Shell Sorting

11

9

8

8

4

Page 24: Missing Link
Lobster

Page 25: Shining Bright

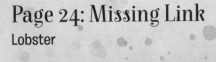
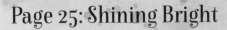

Answers

Page 26: Lost and Found
C

Page 27: Watery Words
Some of the words you could have found were:

ADD

AID

DEN

HEARD

HIDE

RUST

SHUT

SIDE

SURE

STAND

THERE

THREE

TURN

Page 30: Starry Night

Page 31: Seadoku

Page 32: Mermaid Song

Page 33: Odd Otter Out
C - the tail is curling a different way.

Pages 34-35: Mer-map
1 2

2 5C

3 A whale

4 A

5 4B

6 A whale

7 No, 4B and 5B

8 Column 1

Page 36: Crab Course

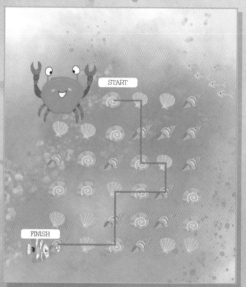

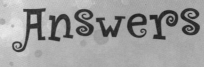

Answers

Page 38: Magical Unicorns

Pages 44-45: Find the Friends

Page 41: Tangled Tiaras

12

Page 42: Mirror, Mirror

c

Page 46: Splash!

Page 48: Finders Keepers

Answers

Page 49: Criss Cross
D

Page 50: Otter Spotter

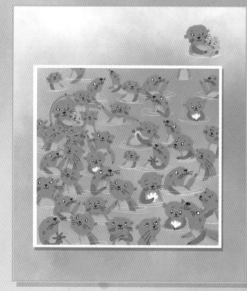

Page 51: Super-search

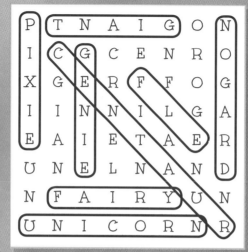

Page 52: Ring, Ring!
D

Page 53: Bubble Trouble

Page 54: Gem-tastic

Page 56: Time for Bed

92

Answers

Page 57: Twinkly Tiaras

Page 62: Shell Seeker

Page 66: Unique Fish

Page 58: Magical Music
B

Page 59: Pretty Patterns

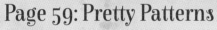

Page 64: Celebrations
C

Page 65: Party Time

Page 68:
Remember, Remember

1 Squirrels
2 2
3 A, C
4 A bird
5 A
6 Fairies
7 C
8 White

Answers

Page 69: Treasure Trove

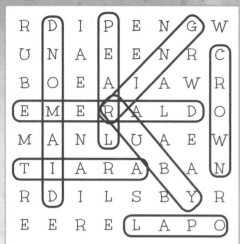

Page 70: Ocean Rescue

Page 73: Sort It Out

A 3

B 2

C 1

Page 74: Giddy Up!

D

Page 75: Watch Out!

Pages 76-77: Mer-map

1 Dolphin

2 2A

3 2

4 3B

5 Row D

6 Unicorns

7 4D

8 5E

Page 78: Scaredy Fish

Answers

Page 80: I Love Mermaids

Page 83: Help for Kelpie

Page 86: Pearl's Purse

Page 82: Sea Tridents

10

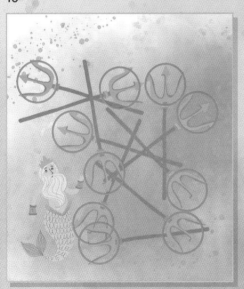

Page 84: Cute Shell-fie

We hope you enjoyed this magical adventure!